'All About'

Louis George Martin

About this collection

This collection of 32 poems was written over the course of a single weekend's cruising from Bristol harbour to Saltford on the river Avon aboard the wide-beam canal boat *'Goldberry.'*

A fine and very merry 2 nights and three days spent with the best of friends.

I hope you enjoy my avant-garde, psychedelic, pseudo-nonsensical, humorous, spiritual poetry.

Please don't take anything too seriously.

I write as I live, and I try to say it true, and that is all.

The poems herein

1. Waiting to cruise
2. A boat load of nymphs
3. Chequers Inn at Hanham Way
4. Aye aye captain!
5. Cruising
6. Forever in the sun
7. The dragon fly darts
8. Coming up
9. River haiku
10. Zen for a moment
11. Twisted ankle
12. Do you put on sunscreen
13. Divine boat leanings
14. Rewind thirty seconds
15. In the grrrrooove
16. Inspire me
17. Lost and found
18. Circular economy
19. So help me god, Mary Jane
20. Sourflake
21. Tentacle porn
22. Tobacco Charlie
23. There a devil inside of me
24. The high story
25. Tell her
26. Take me now
27. I love you
28. The end of the night
29. Another line of K
30. Yawning at the keys
31. Forever bro
32. Standing naked

Waiting to Cruise

I have loved this harbour since before I was born,

The gaily painted canal boats strung along the quayside like a festive lantern,

'sea sharp,' 'spirit of freedom,' 'miss demeanours', 'Albion,' 'redshanks,' 'the flower of Bristol,'

Name a child or your house, sure, a pet,

But naming a boat?

Pure freedom.

It's your god damn boat.

Banked up against a little enchantment,

Your place or mine?

At the end of a long day's cruising, two boaters find solace in the loneliness of each other's arms.

And why not?

Have breakfast on the little deck among the potted plants,

Smoke hash and sunbathe before retiring below deck to the cabin for another tête-à-tête.

The waterways shall forever glisten in the moonlight,

Bright ripples of peace and quiet,

Eddies of pure, whispered joy among the weeds.

Ah, the brown lesser spotted gulls,

The otters and the cormorants,

What gay camaraderie,

At least on a summer's day,

England –

You old dog in heat,

Lie back and have your belly rubbed,

It's time for tea and cake, I say.

A boat load of nymphs

A man's got a right,

After all these lonely nights, spent,

After long days working for the good of –

Dreaming of a little honey,

Some sweet rum and sugar,

Over easy,

Ice and lime to make it.

Got a hole in this here heart ya see,

I'm a leaky vessel taking on water,

And, frankly speaking, the best thing to keep me afloat would be a crew of nymphs and strippers,

It's scorching hot out on the water,

No shade for comfort,

And bucketing out that waters sweaty work

It's only practical to wear nothing at all,

Or at most bikinis, swimsuits, and sarongs,

Aye, that's the life for me –

Captain of my own vessel crewed by nymphs and strippers –

No man could ask for more,

Everyman deserves to make it back upon the shore,

After a dreamy spell on the waterways of the lonely hearts and oft bereft,

Sipping margaritas and saying goodbye,

To another member of the crew –

Retired, quit, done for –

I don't know...something about worker's rights???

Chequers Inn at Hanham way

By the 'Old Lock and Weir Ale and Cider House,'

The morning on the river is quiet, but the traffic steadily grows,

Walkers, drinkers, children, boaters,

Getting merry on the water,

Drinking too much wine and smoking until we pass out,

Writing the bohemian beatnik vibe,

Just late nights with good folk,

Fun musical and poetic folk,

All too talented, too beautiful,

Cruising the river –

It's quite full here,

Can we raft next to you?

Pulling up at this riverside pub for lunch,

These hidden gems of the South West's waterways,

Emerald marinas in golden afternoon sun,

A living relic from an industrial age –

This land we call the United Kingdom –

Such magnificent canals,

The scores of labourers…

Abandoned on completion for the railway.

Aye aye captain!

If I say cast off you know what that means,

She be getting under way,

Rum and smokes all round,

Knots I tie come undone,

I didn't have to pass any test to take this boat out,

That's a 2-day mooring, aye aye!

Saw the grey herons at Saltford lock, and beautiful cranes too,

The river Avon still supporting life,

Vastly intricate network of trees that all drink from it –

The forests connected all the way along,

Weeping willows,

Big old chestnuts, drinking…

It's the things we do more than anything,

Going through Saltford lock,

Keeping the Weir well to our right,

Spectators stand and ogle at our progress,

And at me, dressed in white,

George and J doing all the work,

Damn ankle.

This lock is in the middle of a pub,

So it seems,

Oh shit!

I let go of the rope.

Cruising

Cruising the rivers, the radiant forested highways,

There's freedom on the waterways,

A pirate's escape,

The good life for anyone who can get at it,

Pristine summer days drifting by in a haze,

Meandering along in our own time,

Basking in the glow of nature,

Uncovering the secrets that can only be reached by boat,

This boatmen's crew,

Reed banks, meadows, and city ports,

Aye, it's the pirate's life for me,

Drinking in the blue sky and white fluffy clouds,

Sky and tonic please,

Hard at the helm!

Sharp bends, sunken trees, low bridges,

Reflect in the water,

This wealth of green,

This sumptuous emerald river,

Wending in a boatman's paradise,

On a sunny, summer's afternoon.

Forever in the sun

Forever in the sun

The eternal breath of dying youth,

Taking in the minutes while the houses while on by,

Dragging our feet, not wanting to leave the party, forever digging,

Hoping to be made of steel,

The rattles of a generation;

Grandmother clanging on the chimney pipe with a hammer,

Drunk on cheap champagne,

Aviators and Raybans,

Front row seats to the end of the world,

Highlining, mainlining,

You name it, we're there!

The dragon fly darts

Skimming across the air,

Magnificent, shimmering jewels,

Light as a feather,

As deadly as a dragon fly,

These ancient, armoured dragons,

Ducking and diving in their winged quests,

Such splendid beasts,

See how they dart and move as if by magic,

The blur of their wings a constant hum,

Ah, dragon fly,

Ya be skimming over the water,

And no finer sight.

Coming up

Little fish, little fish,

Breaking the surface tension of the silky water with your plip and your plop,

You disappear as fast as you come up,

but for a moment,

your aquatic underwater world kisses mine,

And I'm cackling in the dusk.

River haiku

Mirrored glassy sky,

Flowing on down the Avon,

Rivers f' wondering.

This river's so slow,

Thank god, we have got all day,

Such sunny idling,

Zen for a moment

A little statue of Buddha

Sitting in his pretty garden by the river,

A thousand blessings in the gentle murmurings of the river,

This moment worth everything,

The same as every other.

Twisted ankle

I twisted my ankle on a parallel line,

Things be jonesing and I ain't know the reason why,

Had it all mapped out,

Now I'm trailing kerosene,

A one man aircraft going down,

May day,

May day,

This is an existential crisis.

I got on board the boat today,

And I could've sworn my intentions were good,

Ended up a one leg pirate,

Pissed as one and all,

A bottle of wine is good if not for nothing,

being followed up with jollies of course,

The harbour master was a grand fellow,

Let us sail the city, chill, and all free of charge.

I twisted me ankle on a Bristol canal,

Somewhere by Beeses tea rooms,

Was rum and a joker till that hazard me down,

Now I'm slip and I'm slumber and suddenly hunkered down,

What a day, what a scorcher,

Burnt my feet and all,

Blisters from dancing on the hot pavement,

Never on my life I swear to god,

I was dancing on my toes for the heat of this sidewalk,

And that's when I got drunk, high,

Stumbled into the cabin,

Drunk and disorderly, but oh, so much fun x

Do you put on sunscreen?

Do you put on sunscreen and stuff?

I do.

I do have the French ability to tanning.

It's not the best, but it's ok.

Why, you're burnt?

I'm white but burnt,

The one and the many,

The many is within the one,

And the many is within the one mic drip.

Divine boat leanings

Shit!

I love Rita –

I'm kind of afraid of heights –

You'll be fine,

We can talk you through the navigation,

I'll be your eyes!

I think this way though J:

You drive on the right,

How in most countries you drive on the left.

But you go in the right, apparently,

This boat doesn't drive itself,

Although, it kind of does,

It kind of does.

Rewind thirty seconds

Something about your legs

Buckled on lands,

A hundred years on the river, still searching,

Questing ever more,

Eye roll.

But seriously,

Why am I here?

I am hungry for all that canal life has to offer,

Follow Sophia,

For she is the goddess of knowledge,

Philos-sophis!

All I want is to know!

The meaning of this vessel with which we dwell,

Life!

I think Kali is on the move,

You'ew insane,

Totally insane,

I know, right?

Isn't it great!

In the grrrroove

None of us have the full package,

And I could get out now,

But we are all just meddling through,

But that's the real shit,

And I could get out of the groove,

But I am just so in the groove,

The fucking groove man,

I'm just right on in there,

And yeah, I probably smoke weed most days,

And I could get out of that,

But I'm just so so in there,

My new website is going to be called enlightened addict.com

It's so hard to be a drug addict and enlightened,

I can't remember what I said,

Oh my god.

People can't understand,

As if it wasn't hard enough to be enlightened, try being a pot smoker as well,

Especially when you have two high grade weeds in jars,

Amnesia, that's what I'm going to try now,

Because I probably want to forget…

Inspire me

Your smile –

My body, a lightning rod –

Lights me up like the Eiffel Tower on a stormy night.

You get me going when I'm feeling bleak,

You are my ultra-high definition,

And you make all my ideas better.

I love you, friend,

The beauty of your song inspires me,

And I am so glad that you are here with me.

Lost and found

I could be lost, or I could be found.

I'm such a reprobate –

I just choose the word emerging

Are you lost, or are emerging?

Emerging?

Have you re-emerged?

I feel I'm on the verge of the merge,

A re-emergence may happen,

I look to the darkness within,

Because within that darkness is the glimmer,

And I am the centre of that glimmer.

The darkness looked upon me,

Within the glimmer,

Forever, whenever,

And ever and ever,

I tied my shoelace and wept, for it was as meant to be.

Circular economy

Life – the complete opposite of a zero-sum game;

The more you give, the more we all have to enjoy,

We all live in a circular economy whether we want to or not;

Water flowing through your body – you are a part of the great river,

Slowly sailing gently on down the stream,

Each day marvelling, pretending, yet disbelieving, it's a dream,

She said these words to me, and I'm repeating them back to you now,

Yet the lineage of this conversation goes back thousands of years,

Carrying the torch from one moment into the next is the breath,

The stream of consciousness flowing in the great river of time,

As you breath, the trees breath,

the whole world breaths together as one, I pray.

So help me god, Mary Jane

For the love of god,

Mary Jane,

Won't you hold me close tonight?

I get such teachings from you,

I swear, space mamma,

And so, what am I saying?

I'm making excuses –

But I shouldn't.

Should just give you the love you deserve,

Same what all sweet ladies deserve,

Putting your fine end in my mouth,

And drawing you deep inside.

Sourflake

That's the god's honest truth,

To categorise means to accuse,

And isn't this curious, given the world we live in and what incessant obsessions there are around categories and the naming of people according to their category,

this and that,

I'm anti this –

I'm a flesh hack and do what you will out of it, I gotta say,

Do it with whoever you wish,

And your category had remained unchanged,

According to some, that is a right-wing view,

But they wouldn't know a thing.

Tentacle porn

I walked in on my French exchange student,

He couldn't close the windows fast enough,

Tentacle porn,

He was drawing it on his PC –

Graphic design.

When I say tentacle porn, you know what I mean?

I'd have sex with an alien in VR –

Wouldn't you?

You need the i-yoni add on,

I've got the i-yoni 3.0,

The tentacles squirt lubricant,

And one of them goes inside your ear.

Tobacco Charlie

This fucked up kid – his mother smoked all through her pregnancy. No way was she stopping for little Charlie. Oh, you should of seen him. How deformed he came out. The cigarette companies denied it. His own mother denounced him. No one could look at him but shudder. He smokes all day long, face like a dried prune. He's only 13 years old. He's only 13 years old…

There's a devil inside of me

"When I see things that's inside of me" –

"Don't fucking give a narrative,

Just fucking discern!"

"But It's better to live in the perfection of the idea,

Because then I don't have to fail,

I don't have to make the imperfect version of perfection,

That's where I'm at,

Calling out my bullshit Lou,

It's like turning a container ship,

It takes awhile…"

The high story

Let's take a moment to acknowledge the duality,

if all I had was a bit of intent and oneness,

Striving from the myness to the duality,

The elemental forces dance at the centre of every atom and every molecule of every fiction –

That is reality,

Which is mostly space,

Each subatomic particle near suggestion?

I enjoyed that one,

A mere suggestion changed everything –

I swear that's the god given truth,

You heard it here,

This is the new reality taking centre stage,

Drip feeding your eyes like holograms say what??!!

Devils spike the atomic structures of your drink,

And then you're coming home with me like what???

Mmmmm.

It's candy crush time.

Sunday in bed baby, let's not get up at all.

Tell her

Two ladies left the boat,

You've made it to the midnight moat,

Surrounded by angles,

If only I could gloat about being a remote boat,

But I only sit and look up at the boat,

Whose gloating now?

I feel like she must be on top...

I have powers of deduction,

She's just nesting,

Rita started speaking to the sky,

Powers of deduction,

What powers of deduction...

Take me now

Take me now, oh spirit of the river,

Swallow me whole, and wrap me in your tender embrace,

I want to feel your slender limbs caress me,

Your watery hold,

Divine water nymphs dancing on your banks,

The hypnotic sway of their hips,

On which we drift,

The tide of love resurgent again,

Keening in the bowsprit,

To be held by this spirit of this river as I sleep,

The Avon,

Loving me, so that I am not alone tonight.

I love you

Falling in love with you was the greatest heart ache I never knew,

It's been a long time since you held me,

And we whispered close as lovers –

Baby don't forget my arms,

And the look I held for you,

The slender touch of open palm across your bare white skin,

To hold you tight to my bosom as a darling bud,

To wed you in the moment of whole soul union,

Take up this cause, I beg of thee,

Forget all wrongs that came before,

Only love me here today as I love you,

So help me god I swear it's true,

And that terrifies the hell out of me…

The end of the night

At the end of the night,

When all the drinks have been spilled,

Steering our way through the Avon canals,

Drifting down forgotten waterways,

I feel brave as a saint,

Despite the bottle of wine, beer, cocktails, and marijuana,

Suppose this makes me a lay about,

Channelling that drunk ass monkey –

Pure Bukaswki.

Only thing worse, Bukawski wannabe,

Slinging shots in the dark,

Eggs breaking windows,

Knock knock, whose there?

The ghosts from our childhood still haunting these desperate hours,

Where long forgotten nursery rhymes take us back to places we never thought we would inhabit again,

Drifting into deep contact with that loving inner child, being span out again on the colour wheel, a different shade,

Pigment 102, vermillion. Most poetic colour ever. Full stop.

The drivers of the night are pure,

Cardinal forks of existence,

Split between us as we are there's so little to go around,

In drunken debauch we share what we can,

Drunk as fell ponies whinnying across the moor.

Another line of K

I could do half a gram right now before k-holing,

It's nothing to be proud of,

my mate, Donor, a big k dealer, was driving,

He snorts a line at 80 mph,

And then I snort the other half,

His tolerance is not going to touch the sides,

These people would do gram lines straight up their noses,

That's what they needed – their tolerance,

And then your kidneys, bladders, and liver all have to deal with that;

It's like a thousand knives in your body,

Friends in their twenties being told you have the bladder of an 80 year old,

That transcendental high that ketamine gives you –

Peeing in a bag –

But it's good fun,

I can't lie,

It's good fun.

Yawning at the keys

Yawning. Nodding off.

Staring down at the keys, trying to avoid the glare of the screen,

Just touch typing and trusting that it's all coming out right,

Midnight is bittersweet, tastes like getting hooked on elven candy,

She's spiced rum, velvet wine, a banquet just for one –

And everything in between.

Poet prays before bed,

Adding diligently to the stack of papers on the desk,

Each day punctuated with these midnight tasting rice crackers –

I paint my poems in peanut butter on rice cakes.

My engine runs on midnight oil –

Burning it at both ends?

How else would I keep moving??

Forever Bro

When you speak English for me it's total nonsense,

I can't connect the dots,

We're being playful,

This is playful,

And he, and they, saw that it was good.

He and they, because it was good,

Huhuhuhuhjbuh,

Metamorphosising like the dervishes,

Twirling like the dervishes,

Was the first step I took when there were no more steps to take,

My particles shattered into ether,

Breathed in by faceless beins,

Ghost, of what was, and what might be,

Forever more and fkrver less,

Amen.

Standing naked

I'm teetering on the brink myself,

Stroking the lip of the abyss,

yet I truly believe in the power of community, how we all lift each other up,

Those who've got broad shoulders,

Get dealt the shit you need to deal with,

To become rock gods,

Every time I bullshit someone it bites me on the arse,

Then I have to sit with that,

We're all oblivious, anyway.

Letter of thanks

To my dear friend J, who owns and lives on a canal boat. You have fulfilled my life-long dream of cruising England's waterways. Though you were almost 5 hours late to pick me up, you did arrive in great style with a crew of 4 women on board, and you literally brought the party to me. And while I was only invited for the one night, after I twisted my ankle, you let me stay the whole weekend until I was well enough to walk off the boat, during which time you cared for me, fed me, and supplied me with copious connoisseurs weed. You are also hilarious company, a deeply poetic legend, and a bloody good egg.

To the crew of the boat, my friends Rita and George, that was fun. I don't get drunk all the time, even though it might seem that way in my poetry, and we do need to let our hair down once in a while, don't we? I love that we can be spiritual healers and a bunch of jolly good humans too. You are some of the best that ever were, and if we stay friends I shall thank my lucky stars.

To the beautiful river Avon, I'd marry your water nymph daughters in a flash and make gorgeous babies left right and centre. May your currents stay strong and your spirit live on, you are fun, you are peace, we are one.

To my readers, I hope you enjoyed this random little odyssey. As always, deeply grateful that you would take the time to read and support my work. Loving you always.

Yours faithfully,

Louis George Martin.

Printed in Great Britain
by Amazon